Intersection at Rose Blvd

Written by Allison Purifoy

Leeron Morraes | Tahlonna Grant
illustrator | editor

ISBN: 978-1-950471-08-9
ISBN-10: 1-950471-08-X
Library of Congress Control Number: 2019947610

No part of this book may be reproduced or transmitted in any form or by any means, electronic or mechanical, including photocopying, recording, or by any information storage or retrieval system, without permission in writing from the publisher. www.beansproutbooks.com

BEANSPROUT BOOKS LLC
Morongo Valley, California
2019

I'm longing for your call
the seconds are ticking
my mind is racing
just to hear your voice
would make everything okay

we always get to that point where we start drifting
I'm not going to let that happen again
I'll do everything I can to keep you close
and safe this time

I don't care what it takes
this time we're going to make it
this time we are going to be okay
and that's a promise

The Dreamer Awoke

I was waiting for "the one"- a lunatic
                        some would say
Apparently I'm not that significant
I followed him relentless
Crazy fools we may be
what we put ourselves through
on and on
on and on
day in and day out

day in and day out again...

You left in such a rush
you haunt me in my dreams
as I lay here in this bed
my fingers remember this place
we sat arm in arm in chatter
until it came time and the
dreamer awoke

In All Honesty

I'm hoping it's just a phase you're going through
wanting to break through, break loose from everything we created
They don't know you like I know you, they just assume the worst in all you do
But me, I try to see hope

I distract myself-praying things get back together some way
Hoping love will conquer everything that exists between us
Everything that separates us from time and each other
I believe in you and me and no matter how bad things seem to get
just know I'm not perfect, but I'm trying my best
I know sometimes I lose control and put myself in the worst of situations
but it's because I love you and in all honesty, I'm scared to death of losing you

Thank You

I lost you out there, when I said the wrong thing
You left before I could apologize, took flight with those wings
With your skin so pale, you'll blend right in
And I'll keep searching, end to end

You said "I love you", but I hesitated
You caught me off guard
I shouldn't have waited
and when the words came out,
all I could say was, "thank you, I didn't
know you felt that way"

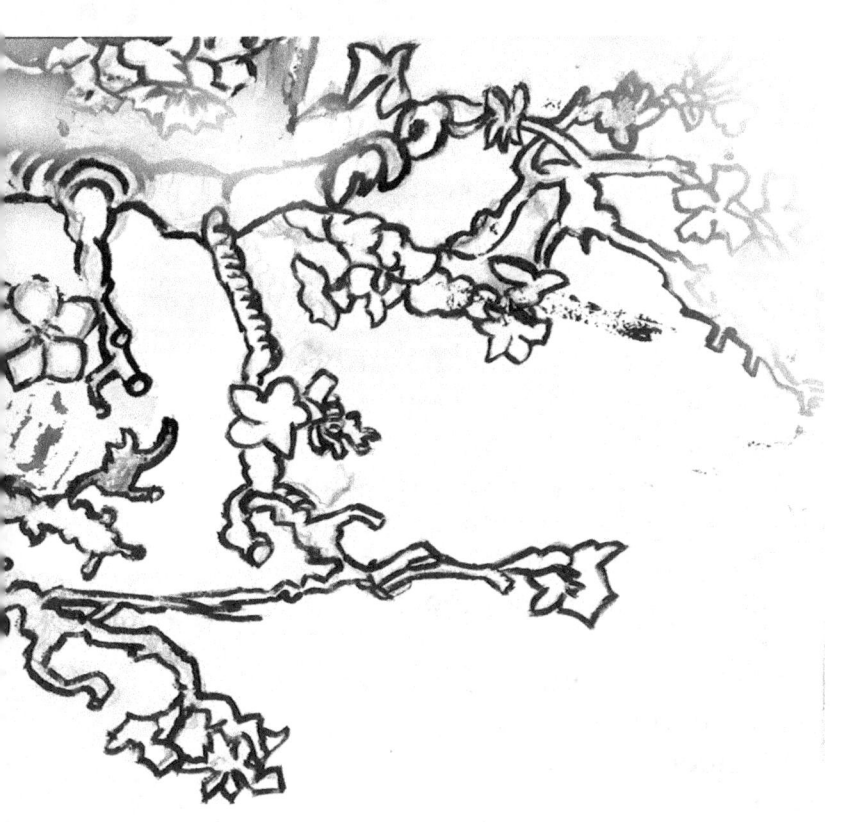

And now you're gone
and I'm falling apart
Do I love you, with all my heart?
The night is young, but cold as ice
I'm worried to death I won't find you tonight

I fall to my knees, the pain is too strong
Now I know I've loved you, all along

She Speaks

It's time to move on she speaks
as he thinks she'll always be around
To catch him, to wait for him,
and wait for the sound
of his voice
to whisper soft-spoken words
instead she gets nothing
and her cries are unheard
Tired of waiting, she softly speaks
Hiding the scars, under her sleeves
He still thinks she's waiting
but she's no longer there
Ending the cycle
because she no longer cares
She stands up proudly
No need for fear
and the sad part is
he has no idea

Haikus

million miles away
no clue of when you'll return
love will have to wait

love is just a sign
that leads to heartbreak and pain
you can bring it on

looking in your eyes
I see myself right through you
no better feeling

Falling Fast

Here I go again...falling fast
Afraid to open up this parachute
Afraid it might be broken
Afraid I won't land safe
but what the hell, I'll open it
I'll give it a try
at least that way I know I tried and I didn't give up
At least I'll know I didn't just sit back and hit the ground
Is it so wrong to finally feel happy, to finally believe in yourself
No, it's not...that's why I'm landing safe and sound

Every Little Thing

You've dug me out of this hole I've been in for so long
You're every little thing I've wanted and more
I don't know how I found you, you just came to me through
a journey, you and I have taken so many times
I guess the thing we love the most brought us together
and thinking about that makes me smile from ear to ear
I'm hoping, I'm wishing, I'm praying
something this good will last
Because this is everything I've ever wanted and more
I know we are miles and miles apart
and our lives get hectic
but just know I don't mind
Because every thing we go through makes me
wanna make it with you, no matter what the obstacles

Life Support

Everything makes sense now,
it was all for the best the way it all happened
Life had to show its misery to me before it let me off easy
It wasn't going to deal me an easy hand
and now I understand
I really wondered how many hits to the heart I could take
how many times my heart could break
I was beginning to think I was invincible
but it still killed me every time, don't get me wrong
Then every time before they pulled the plug
someone would save me, revive me
But their life support just wasn't enough
it never lasted as long as I needed it to
I needed someone flawless to cure me
Someone who knew what they were doing
But it wasn't that easy, I'd grow unconscious every time
dead to the world, dead to love
Then my mind started to build its own shell to surround
what was left of my heart and soul, scared to wake up
scared to come out to feel the pain again
but then, an angel came to save me, and I surrendered
and I've been awake ever since

You Know What They Say

When it rains it pours and damn it's raining hard
everything falling down with it
everything falling out of place
the tears, the memories, the lost
such a heavy weight to carry on those shoulders
adds on about 100 pounds

And just when I thought things couldn't get worse
I thought wrong

The sick are getting sicker, things once new are now old
and so they say it's time for a change
well I'm not ready for a change

Houses going up for sale, memories going out to sail
sailing far, far away

A picture's worth a thousand words
but I'd cry a thousand tears to keep those memories safe
and where they need to be

where they happened
took place
where I was raised and born

They say when you get older you have to be ready for change
I wish I could change…

change back into that seven year old little girl,
whose worries were absolutely nothing…

You Did It

You did it, you finally put a smile on my face
Never thought someone could do that again
but you proved me wrong
I'm falling for you, all of you
All you have to do is catch me
It's just a simple task, not much to ask
I think you can handle it,
and that makes me happier
I'm giving my heart to you
so please, please
don't break it

In the Deep

Your killer injection has set my eyes to sleep
But while I was sleeping, I wandered in the deep
The deep part of nowhere- that lies inside your palms
Where I stand, where I dream, even where I fall

You're taking everything I have
Force it down, it's not so bad
I'd rather die, than live for you
Poison me, you'll find the truth

A Voice with No Voice

Someone wants to hurt me
and bring my spirit down
I feel it deep within my bones
in every waking sound

It pierces through my gut
and I'm forced to believe
The reason that you live
is to sit and watch me bleed

I hope it's not the case
but you leave me with no choice
to say the things I'd never say
even though I have a voice

Bittersweet

Why even try, if we're gonna give up

It's all on the line, enough is enough

I'm not alone, we all feel the same

When push comes to shove

I'm always to blame

It's bittersweet, but all I know

So hard to reach, but I can't let go

I can't say the things that I need to say
Too scared you'll leave and run away
Leave for the better, run from the worse
Everything that I touch seems to be cursed

we grow, we change
we lose our leaves
we bend we break
forget to breathe

we stand so tall
we lose it all
we get back up
refuse to fall

A Race Against Time

I sit on the sidelines
as the world spins away
Time's growing faster
and I'm growing gray
My body grows weaker
and my heart turns colder
Things hold us back
We halt like soldiers
We live in the future
but we're stuck in the past
Just wanting to make it
but time's fading fast
Speed up the process
No time for delay
A race against time
as the world spins away

Lullaby

I'd lay here beside you
to just hear you breathe
like diamonds way up in the sky
You shine just like a ring

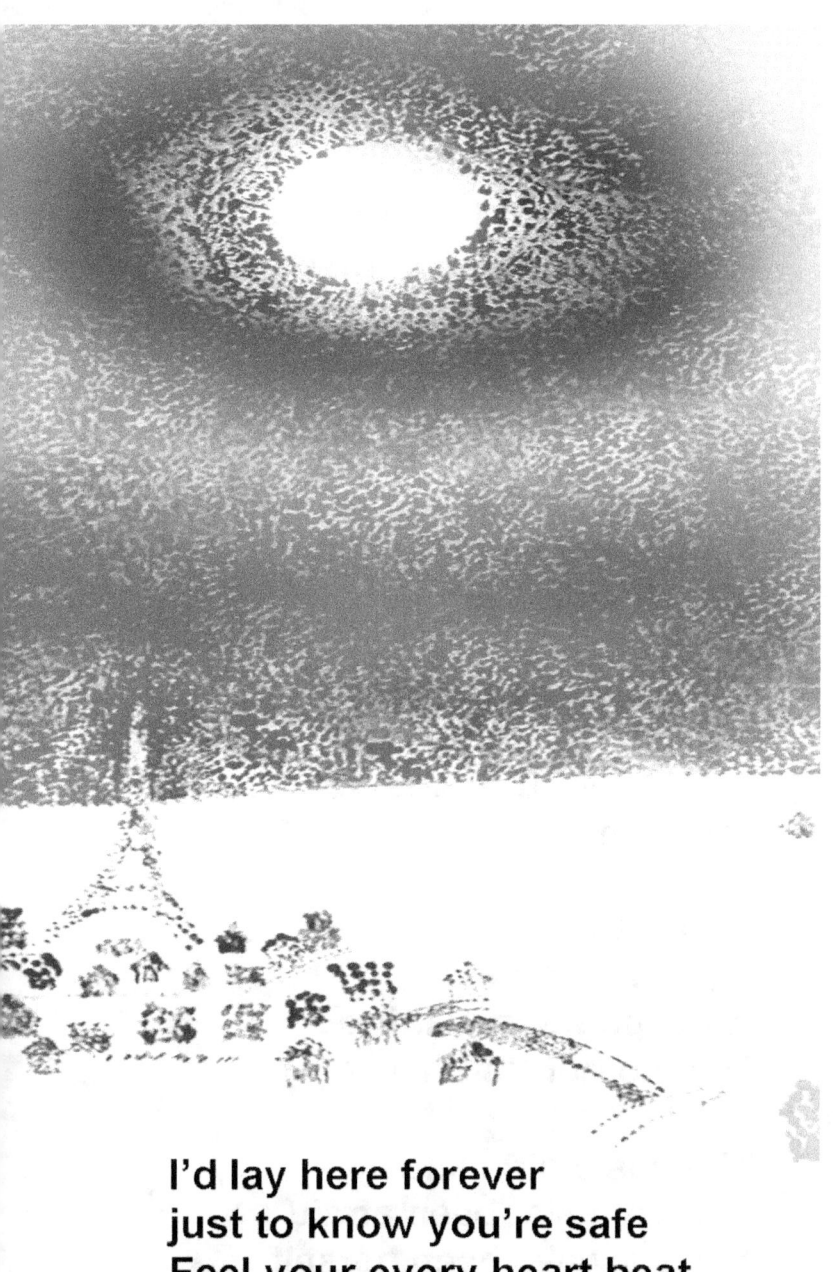

**I'd lay here forever
just to know you're safe
Feel your every heart beat
like the rhythm feels the rain**

Gypsy

There is a girl I know
Who never stays in town
She's always on the go
Like a gypsy in a gown

Wandering in her mind
Looking for adventure
It's her only sane place
It's her only cure

A voyage to the mountains
A trip to touch the sky
The higher that she gets
She thinks that she can fly

A tour to see the stars
A journey-an escape
An expedition waiting
To help her find her fate

There is a girl I know
Whose never been afraid
She's always been herself
Through every path she's paved

Keep your fire burning
with the warmth you store inside
You're strong, you're tough, you're worthy
don't let your beauty hide

Just close your eyes
Breathe in deep
The world will sweep you
off your feet

why do you care so much about someone who cares nothing for you?

'cause you are crazy but so am I

it's funny how people can totally change in one day
totally different than they were the day before

there's so much tension in the room-
I can't think straight
there's so much love in the air
it turns to hate

this is probably gonna hurt
go on and rip me off
like the tape over my mouth

I'm no stranger to misery
The enemy of my enemy is my friend
My demons are my play toys
Reminding me of every sin

Torn

Torn between what's wrong and right
These feelings taunt me and keep me up at night
There's an angel and devil I carry around
They rest on my shoulders and weigh me down
Let it go or hold onto this anger
I've gone too far—-now I'm a stranger
No one knows me, nor myself
Torn into—with nothing left

The darkness smothers me
Takes my breath
The undertaker digs a hole
The silence makes me deaf
They all stare me down
I'm cold like the snow
Dead, but I'm breathing
As they let me fall below

The weak will slowly vanish
The damaged will survive
The wounds will never heal in time
That's how we'll know we're still alive

Lifeline

I put my life on the line

to watch you cut it down

I fall helplessly

as you let me drown

In open waters

I'm nothing but bait

You're looking to kill

But you're way too late

I was already gone

Before you let me go

I put my life on the line

So you'd never know

Oblivion

I stare looking into oblivion
An endless sea of struggle
Was it all for nothing?
As I watch the tide take what remains out to sea

I fall to my knees and the sand scatters
like dust in the wind
All alone with every thought in my mind
Crowded inside like a shell
I'm forced to crawl out

I draw closer and closer
to the water
Waves beat harder and harder
than hands on a drum

I hear my heart no longer
No racing pulse this time
I walk until the waves take me under
I was always afraid of drowning
until now

How do you breathe when you don't want to live
How do you love, when you can't forgive
How do you seek when you choose not to find
what you've always wanted
enclosed in your mind…

Message In A Bottle

If I could peel off the skin
that clings to my bones
You would see broken parts
and a heart so alone

You'd find holes and gashes
from the hits that I've taken
Mistakes from the past
have left me forsaken

Deserted, I'm lonely
Searching for you
But you lead me astray
out in the blue

We've never seemed distant
but at times we've passed by
Until an ocean of turmoil
Made our ships collide

We sank to the bottom
along with the wreckage
like victims we drown
'cause we missed the message

Love one another
no matter the case
Life is too short
You'll lose them some day

And above the surface
among the waves
you'll find one day
the love we saved

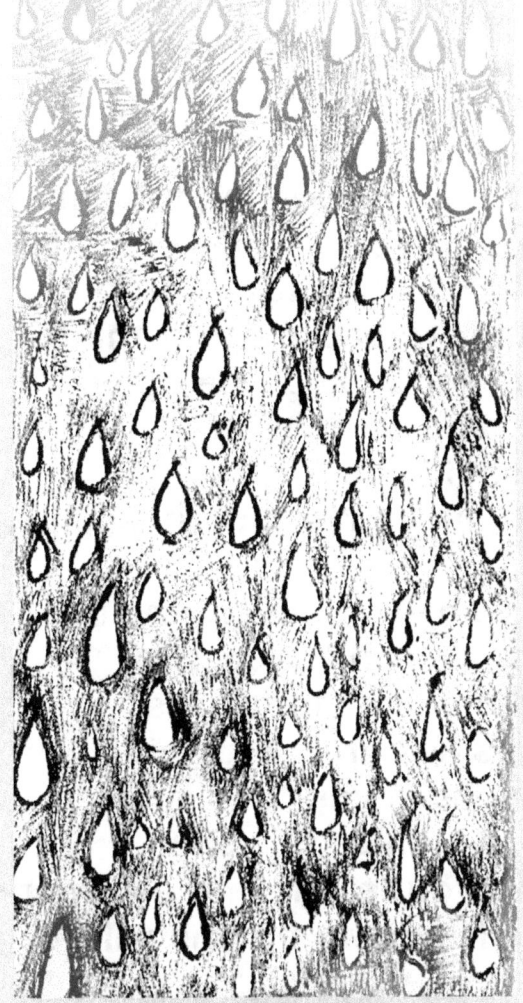

heavy rain,
roaring breeze
wash me out
into the sea
the clouds are angry
crying out
thunder's roaring
no sign of drought

Pretend

There's no reason left to speak
because my words don't matter
You throw them to the curb
like they're background chatter
In one ear and out the other
You value no opinion
Unless it is your own
You think you're **one** in a million

This web you spin around us
Suffocates and squeezes
Leaves us lost for words
Leaves us barely breathing
A recluse in your own mind
Trapped inside this shell
Where you're safe and always right
if you're wrong no one will tell

You live the perfect life
You are a perfect person
You wish that you could clone us
into your own little versions
Speaking a language
You only comprehend
That would be the life right
too bad it's all pretend

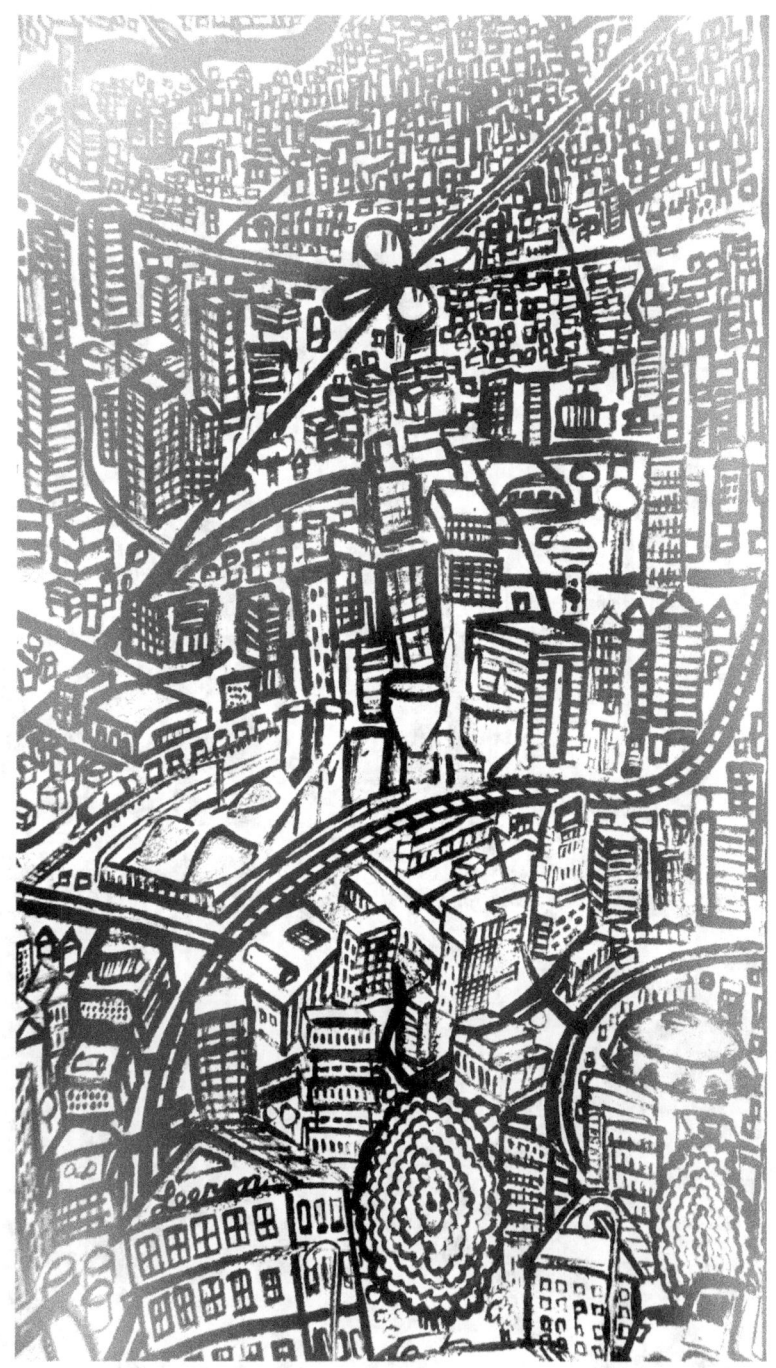

Rain

Pour on me, let me drown
Wear the rain just like a crown
Wear it proud, wear it true
Let the raindrops cover you

Embrace the heat, let it be
I only hope you think of me

Rain on me, let me down
We're still both here, same old town
Wanting to leave, like a ship in the night
The water's rising, I'm not alright

Yet here you are, a sky turned gray
I only hope, that you're okay

Love

Oh the things we do for love
We worship the ground
when we should look above
Misguided, we're clueless
Don't think with our heads
Our hearts play the victims
So they have to play dead
Halting the beat, we have to move slow
So the flame will die down
And lose it's control
We yearn for the passion
we felt in our youth
Young and not restless
With nothing to prove
We cherish the memories
Though they cause us pain
Can't seem to let go
Because we're both to blame

The Perfect Storm

You were the perfect storm
Your calmness pulled me in
You brought the rain down with you
With the thunder and the wind
Roaring with your glory
You let me see the truth
You let me see your rage
The wrath that made you——you
Showering your greatness
I feel it touch my skin
A powerful addiction
I felt you from within
Lighting up the sky
You brought yourself to life
No one could control you
You were too strong to fight
Reigning down on earth
Like royalty adored
I'll crave you every time
Because you leave me wanting more

Brilliance

We all can be radiant
We all can shine through
We all can burn bright
Like the sun and the moon

We all can show greatness
We all can be free
We all can be brilliant
and become anything

We all can stand tall
from nothing at all
We all can dream big
there's no need to stall

We all can be beautiful
We all can fly high
We can light up the world
We just have to try

Will you choose the darkness
like an owl in the night
or will you be a star
and glow oh so bright?

the choice is yours....

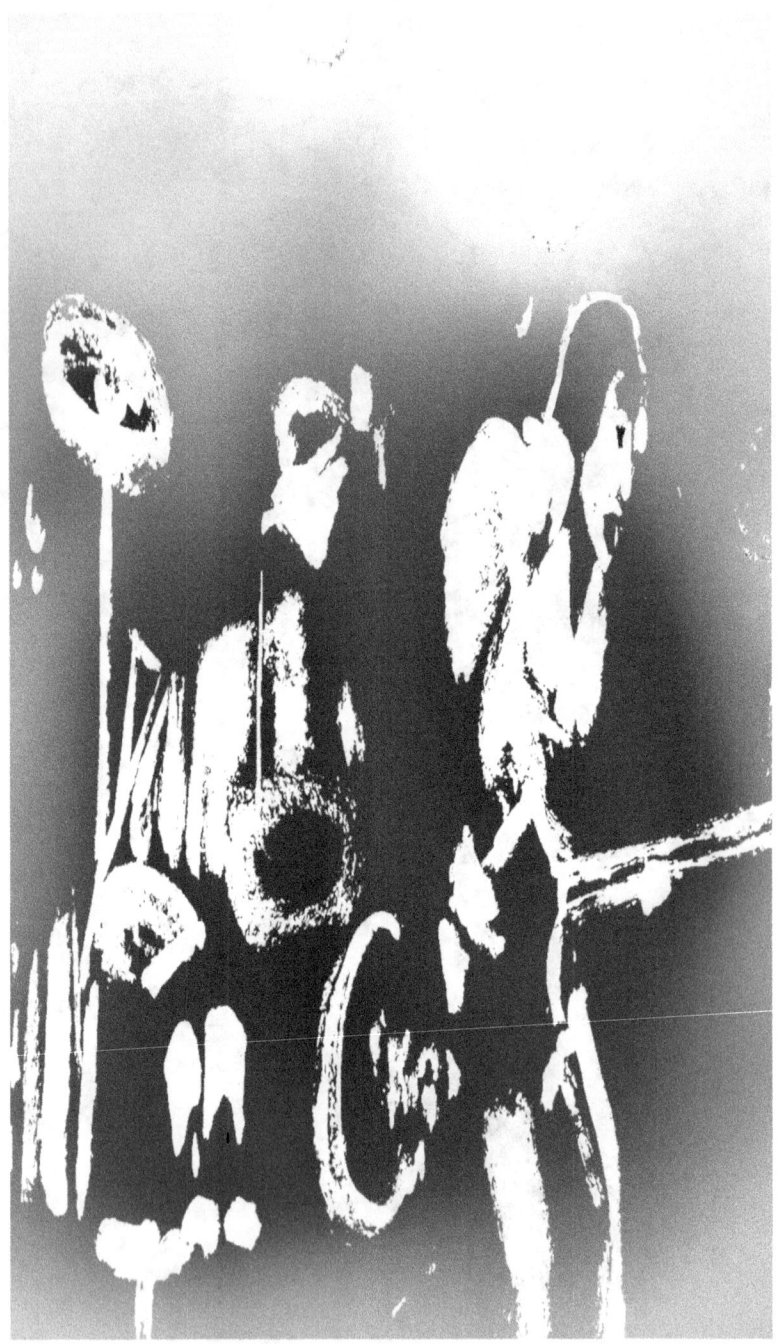

Anger

We let it consume us
Lose our control
A vexation, no pity
with rage in our souls

We lick at our wounds
to hide the disease
There's pain in our eyes
from the lies we believe

This ire——it keeps us
locked in a cage

There's a war deep within us
Consumed by the rage

Forced to live in a world that's dead
We've become monsters
who just want to be fed

Like prey vs. predator
we were born to survive
Yet we still ask the question
Will we get out alive?

Sadness

I am your suffering
I am your pain
I am the fallen
who can't stand the rain

I am your sorrow
I am the night
I am the moon
who can't shine bright

I am the heartache
I am the cold
I am the story
that always gets old

I am despondent
I am dejected
I am the song
that's always objected

I am down hearted
I am despair
I am the love
that was never there

Joy

I'm high on the waves
I'm high over sea
I'm up in the clouds
I'm far out of reach

I can feel the rapture
Taking its course
There's bliss in the air
Ecstasy in the smoke

A delightful feeling
No one could ruin
Can't hide from these feelings
Who am I fooling?

More than contentment
Can't hide from the truth
This joy in my heart
Is controlled by my youth

Never grow up, never grow old
Stay true to yourself, don't let the world turn cold
Be high on life, always be free
Like you're high on the waves, high over sea

Fame

You think a lot of your reputation
Standing tall through desperation
No regard, to the ones you've hurt
Wasted fame to see your worth
Immoral values will drag you down
Heavy's the head who wears the crown
Popularity- the biggest lie
A blood sucking nemesis- that will bleed you dry
You have to acknowledge your surrounding walls
They show the pictures, relive your withdrawals
You're pathetic, a no one, who couldn't buy fame
Couldn't repute, couldn't rename
You'll always be you, fortune aside
Always renowned, because you couldn't abide

Wishes

It wasn't my intention to ever cause you pain
I hope you will forgive me, like the sun forgives the rain
I'm longing for the day, when things will be okay
Yearning for the answers, yet always changing lanes
My desire has me clouded, the future is unclear
Ambition is the devil, when you're scared to face your fears
I know my dreams are **waiting**
can almost touch them with my hands
Yet my only aspiration, was to hope you'd understand
It was never my intention, to ever bring you pain
I wish you could forgive me, because I accept the blame

Fire

Flicker, flicker
little flame
Burn inside and feel my pain

You're my hearthstone
You're my home
Burn the skin-expose the bone

Your smoke is poison
Can't take one breath
A lasting flare, when nothing's left

Crackle, crackle
little fire
Reach inside and burn the liar

Night Sky

Moonlight madness
you and me
A midnight canvas
we only see
We are the stars that light the sky
Our own constellation
resisting time
We glimmer in darkness
but hide in the day
We wait for the blackout
then come out and play
A wakeful evening
we embrace the night
The moon is our friend
it's the sun to our shine
The blackness will cover
the clouds in the sky
And the sun will sleep tight
Just knowing you're mine

Imperfection

I am the imperfection
a flaw within the seams
A blemish on a pretty face
a nightmare in a dream

I am the distortion
the static in the channel
A search within the atmosphere
I guess I'm hard to handle

I am a force of nature
a hurricane on land
Destroying all that's beautiful
no footprints in the sand

A defect in my code
I'll never add up right
It's your fault for believing
that I would be alright

You can change me all you want
why is it hard to see
I'm just too far gone
but I always will be me

Insecurity

I've exposed myself
for the world to see
Showing my colors
and flaws underneath
A fear of uncertainty
a need to belong
An endless struggle
the day is long
If I live in doubt
I'll never live
Just use caution
try to forgive

myself….for the things I can't relive

The Ocean

Take me out to sea-let the waves enrapture me
Take me high, then bring me low
Into the depths, I'll sink below
I am the ship that's lost direction
and like the anchor, I'll make connection
I'll touch the bottom, see the floor
like hidden treasure, inside the core
But I am the shell, without the pearl
there is no gift, but a lonely girl
That sees the ocean, and feels so small
just waiting for the siren call

Clouds

Fade into the smoke, you don't have to say goodbye
Go out into the mist, like a cloud up in the sky
A disappearing act, your love was always magic
I could feel it in my bones, electricity and static
Swarming like a bee, stinging like a poison
Drinking down your potion, was like poetry in motion
But now the bottle's empty, I drank it down too fast
Just like that cloud up in the sky, I knew it'd never last

Squished

Squished like a bug in a mosh pit
I'm 5 foot one, but my candle's still lit
Standing tall like lady liberty
My poetry book in one hand, not feeling guilty
So overrated, to be so perfect
My words are a guideline, I flow with the current

Dim

This heart inside me grows so weak
I try my best not to sink
My fire's dying, the flame is dim
but just enough, for me to write about him

More Than Beauty

Small, like a butterfly
I'm free, but I can't identify

wish I was greater than what I seem
I'm the beauty, you can't redeem

flying high above the trees
you can't catch me, you can't catch me

The reason I breathe, is to get breathless....

Dares

Dare to dream
high and above
We crave the thrill
of the things we love
The passion builds
it flows through our veins
Drives our hearts
we have no shame

Dare and try
to reach your goal
Fly above
and free your soul
Stand up tall
don't be afraid
Just let destiny
pave the way

the night is quiet
yet I can't sleep
I picture your face
and I feel defeat
My heart, it aches
and longs for you
I reach for your hand
but fall right through

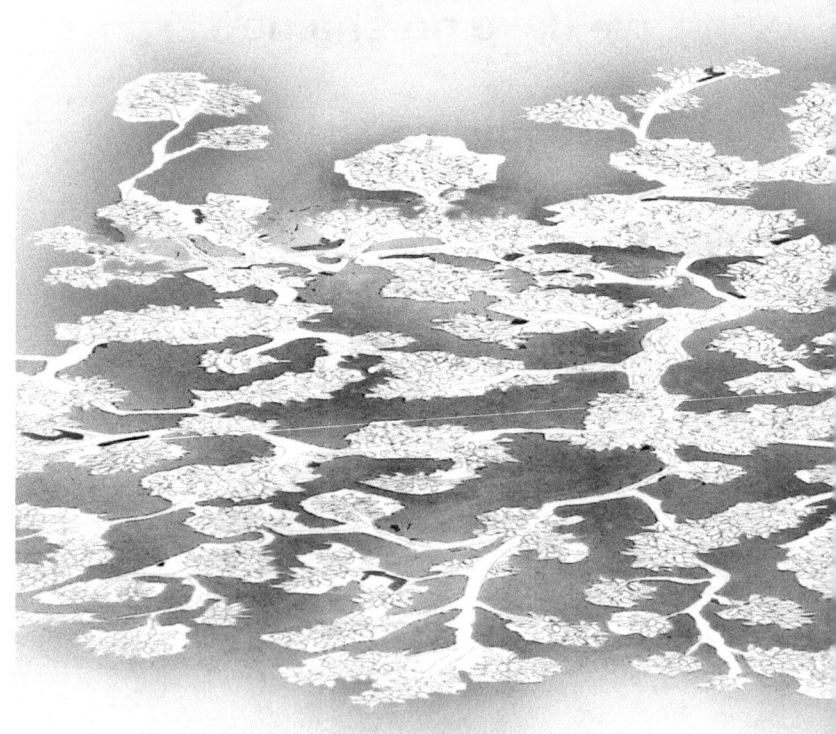

Thorn Bush

I've always been the thorn bush in the rose garden
Pricking the petals, one at a time
and standing there with a sore thumb
It's not how my seed was planted
or how I chose to be
It's the way I grew from the roots
in that cold, hard ground

I always thought I'd be beautiful like the others
anticipating my buds to bloom
but what only grew from that was patience and acceptance
I hid down low so no one could see me

Maybe I was ashamed of how I looked
or maybe I was hiding my jealousy
maybe even embarrassed

All I know is when I almost let my true colors show

My face became red as a rose

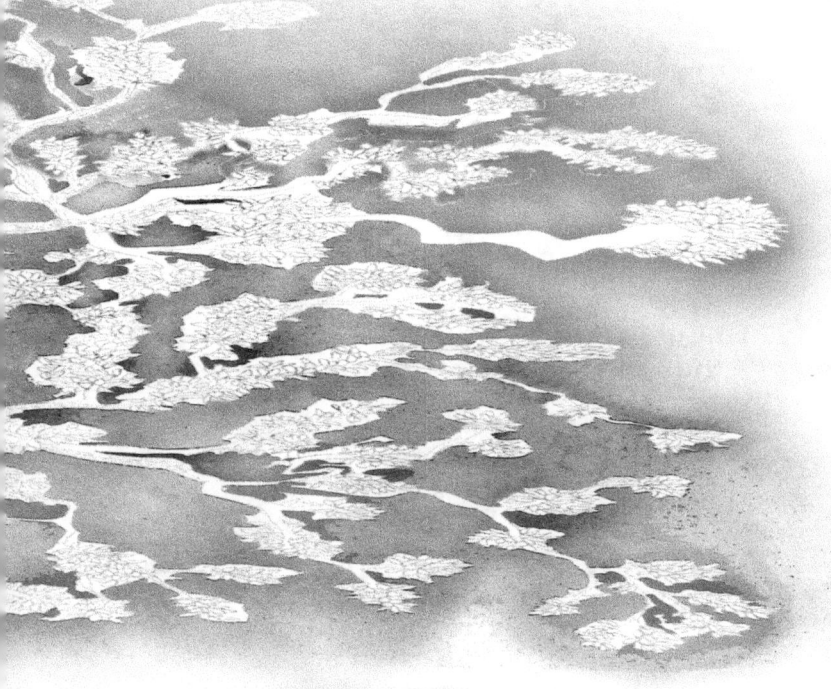

Change

My anger is at rest
My soul is finally free
And now I see the world
Much more differently

The seasons quickly change
And I change with them too
I fall off my branches
then spring back—-good as new

Patience is the key
That opens all the doors
You mustn't hold your breath
If you want to be restored

You must play your part
And know all of your lines
Or you'll turn into something
You cannot define

The beautiful-they don't have to survive
They're looked upon, like souls revived
A burning sun, reflects the light
A moon so bright, it lights the sky

The ugly-we will have to fight
To keep our stance and peace of mind
Faces scarred and filled with fright
Under the mask, yet still too bright

Opinions of the sheep
Exposed to the wolves
They'll eat you alive
with their words
Cut out your tongue
Feed it to fire
Ashes to ashes
we've lost our desire

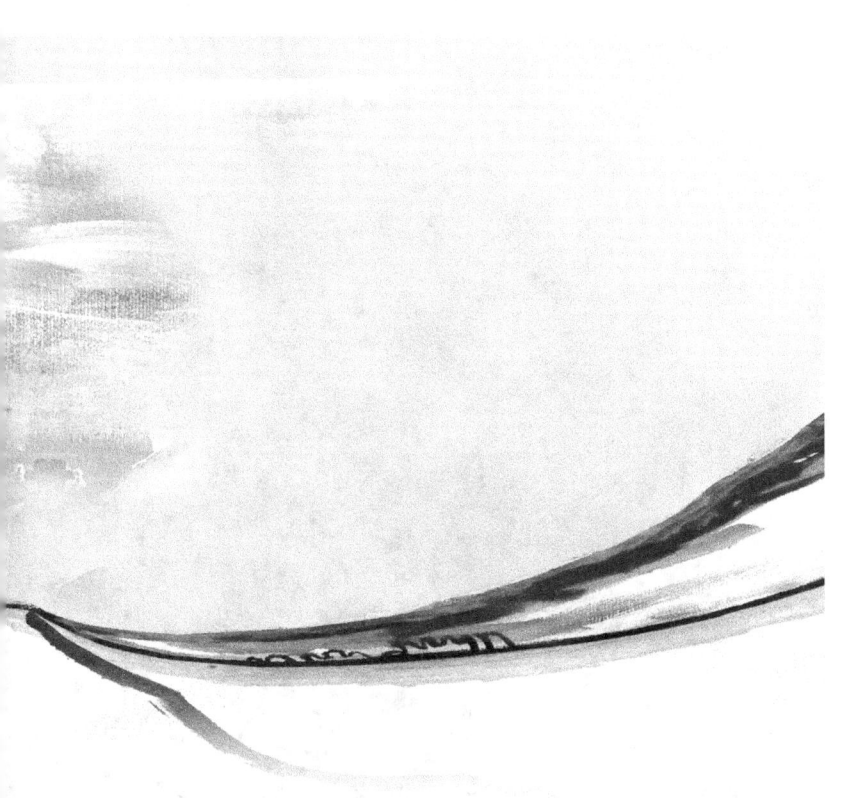

Sail off into the ocean
Hand in hand, a lie
I'll watch from a distance
Laugh and say goodbye
A perfect little moment
Ruined by desire
The ones we love are ghosts
Filthy little liars

I'm slowly realizing
the world's a bitter place
Rethinking all the choices
Some I wish I never made

Where did I lose myself?
Where did I go wrong?

**The mirror, mirror on the wall
Tells the tales of those who fall**

**I hate the face that stares me down
Face the truth, can't turn around**

Half

I knew you'd change way to soon
just like the shape of the moon

Some days I feel you're half way here
Some days your full and you seem near

Why do you hide beyond the clouds
Hiding your bright side, because you feel too loud

So ashamed to show who you are
Just another fallen star

I'm done looking close for help

I'll broaden my horizons

Search deeper

where I've never been before

to find what I need

because it's not here

it never really was

Shell

I'll hide away in this shell
where no one can find me
Pray the sun won't blind me
And when my skin burns off
I pray they won't see
Everything I used to be

But if they do
I won't be the person they once knew
I'll be someone totally new

Perfect Storm

I feel the calming of the storm
A time to change and be reborn
A gentle breeze with a harsh, black sky
Innocence, washed away
until it's dry
I hear the thunder, shake the earth
A renewed existence, my own rebirth
I feel the rain, I feel alive
The tears won't show, when they fall from my eyes
A perfect disguise,
to cover the flaws
to show the truth, bitter and raw
An escape from reality
the chance to be free
Bring on the flood
and wash over me

Will this dream kill me
before I reach it
touch it?

Will I ever see it?
Do I just keep walking
until I see the light?

Where is my tunnel?
Where is the opening?
I can't find it
I can't find it

Lost in the dark
and I forgot my flashlight

Comatose

they almost lost him around yesterday
around midnight

flipped, spun

out of control
he rests comatose
she spills love out of her eyes

Smells Like Lost Spirit

Fringed pom-poms lay in a dusty corner

Where did her spirit go?
Where did her voice go?

Nothing but a hoarse scream
lingering through a broken down gym

she sits down on the bleachers
looks out to an empty floor

and realizes she's just another lost spirit
lingering in the past

Reverse Psychology

My stem reversed
and sunk back into the ground
Defeat crowded me
like sweaty bodies at a rock concert
No room to move
No room to breathe
Existing like another seed
planted in a row
I only saw the light once
and it was beautiful

Grasping Stars
Lying here beside you
In many countless sheets
The satin hits my face
And the air is filled with heat
Your hand is lightly resting
On my body fast asleep
The other's grasping stars
While the mind is counting sheep
A candle's lit beside us
The only warmth that's there
Except the breaths we take
Resting there so fair
Your touch belongs to heaven
Because it's perfect that you're here
Your love is madness
Your love is real

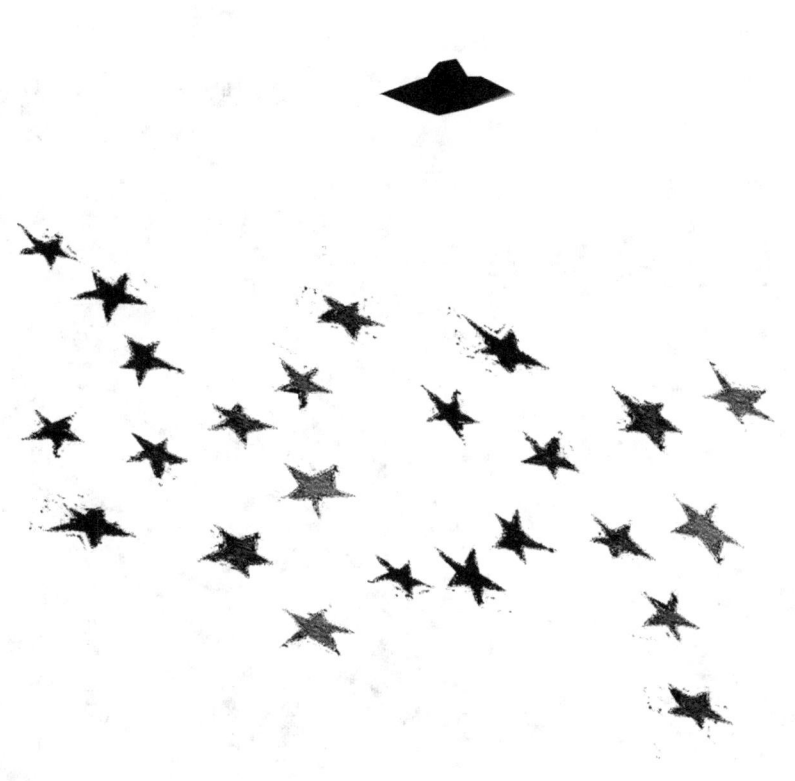

like an alien from another planet
this will never be my home
I belong among the flowers
I am a song unsung

**if the ending doesn't catch you
there's more work to be done**

**if the beginning doesn't start you
you can never run**

secrets don't make friends
they only spawn the enemy

When She Wakes

He's traumatized, she's paralyzed
Her fate resides, unverbalized
Lying still, if looks could kill
Force it down, a bitter pill
If she wakes, you'll kiss the ground
The sweetest taste is always found
Count your blessings, say your prayers
Just to know that you're aware
Good things in life are hard to find
And when they're lost you can't rewind
Hold on tight and don't lose faith
And thank the heavens when she wakes

right or wrong
the truth will be shown
we are all fighting for something
together, yet alone

Captivated

The first time that I saw you,
you cast a spell on me
I was captivated
I couldn't see
You led me in your eyes
I followed you straight down
Hypnotized, by your disguise
I never made a sound

I hate the silence because my thoughts
are louder than my actual voice.
I don't know if I can hold this in any longer,
because it's tearing me apart

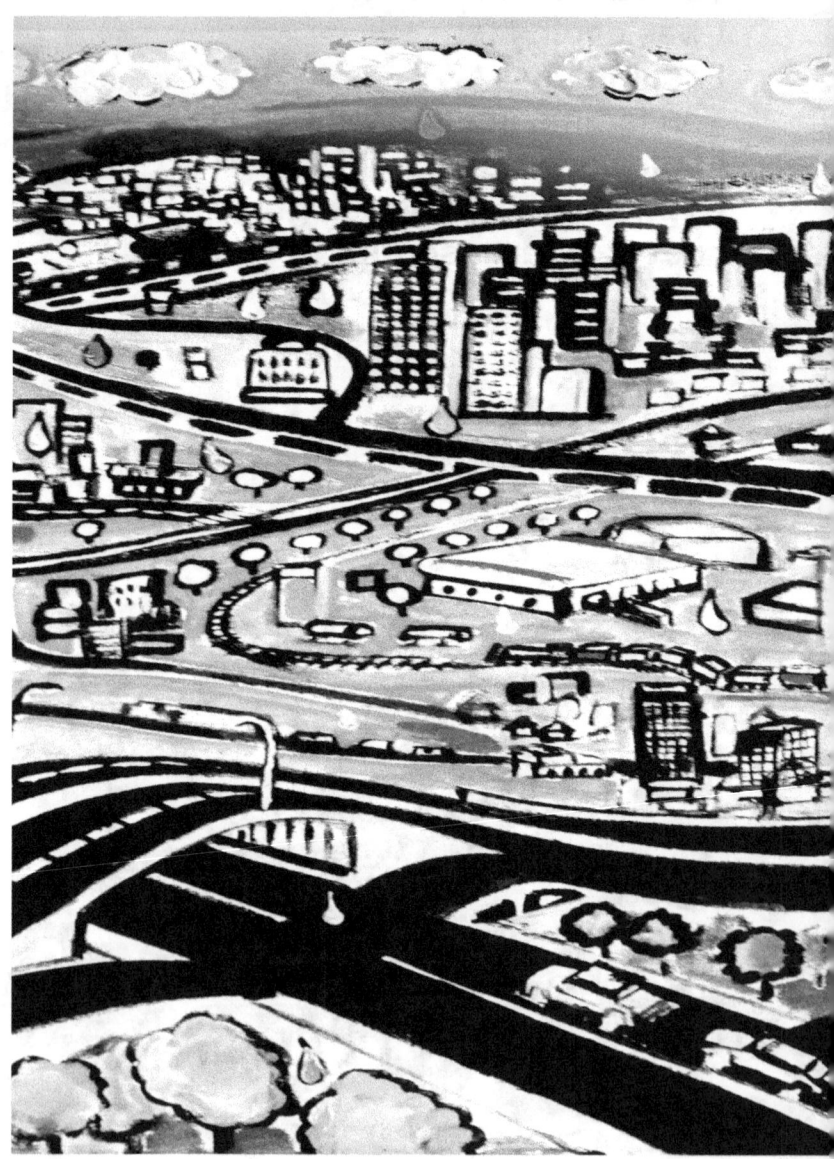

Thoughts
To gain one step
I'll take ten back
Can't please the world
and that's a fact
Prove me wrong
I bet you can't
I'll leave this life
Full of regret
Sometimes I wonder
How I keep going
Every day gets harder
and it just keeps storming
It always rains on my parade
and it's harder and harder
to face each day

I hope you have a restful night
While I'm losing sleep
I hope the angels sing to you
As the demons scream at me

Nothing's ever good enough
And never will it be
If I can't please you
I can't please me

Don't know why you let it get to you
You'll be the last man standing
if it's the last thing you do
Push me away, break me in two
I'm tired of trying to find the truth
It hurts like hell, a sucker punch
To the gut, an easy crutch

You think we'd be used to it by now

You would think….

but it feeds and feeds upon us
like a blood-sucking leech

It's amazing no one can hear the screams I hear inside my own head.

A river of emotions
A song made from waves
Sun beaming on my face
No time for shade

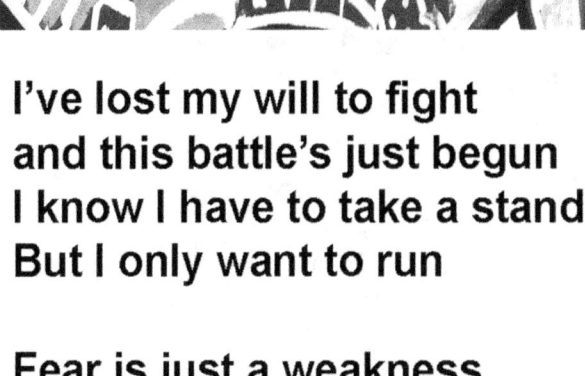

I've lost my will to fight
and this battle's just begun
I know I have to take a stand
But I only want to run

Fear is just a weakness
Failure's all the same
I feel it in my bones
But won't let it call my name

Phobia?

This is no phobia
A guarantee to the 9th degree
We are all blindsided
Scared of reality
An average day to most
But this is an atrocity
Inside we don't settle
Just laugh at mediocrity
Trapped inside our minds
Tenacious to the core
We run from our issues
but never open the door

I've become numb from people leaving me
It's almost like second nature
It doesn't even phase me anymore
I used to cry like a baby
Not anymore
Now I just don't care
It's second nature
it's just a phase
Numb to the tension
With nothing to gain

Numb

there's nothing to fill this void
I feel empty
and my heart hurts

I'm desperate, I get it
I'm stupid for even feeling this way

Am I happy?
Yeah, sometimes

Right now?

I don't know.

I'd be lying if I said I was.

What is….living proof

Silence is deafening
The truth is a lie
Love is a poison
Who wears a disguise

Peace is a weapon
Don't live for the good
We do as we please
Because we're misunderstood

Falling to pieces
We're drifting apart
We think with our heads
Instead of our hearts

Losing control
Drowning in fear
Don't know who we are
or the reasons we're here

Existing and breathing
Living as one
Although separated
We shine like the sun

We think we are perfect
And we're never wrong
Although we are weak
We say we are strong

Madness is sanity
Because we can't face the truth
Don't need the answers
Because we're living proof

I've built up this wall
I can't break it down
Have I lost my way?
Can I ever be found?
I know that you're free
But I'm trapped in this hell
Millions of wishes
Thrown away in this well

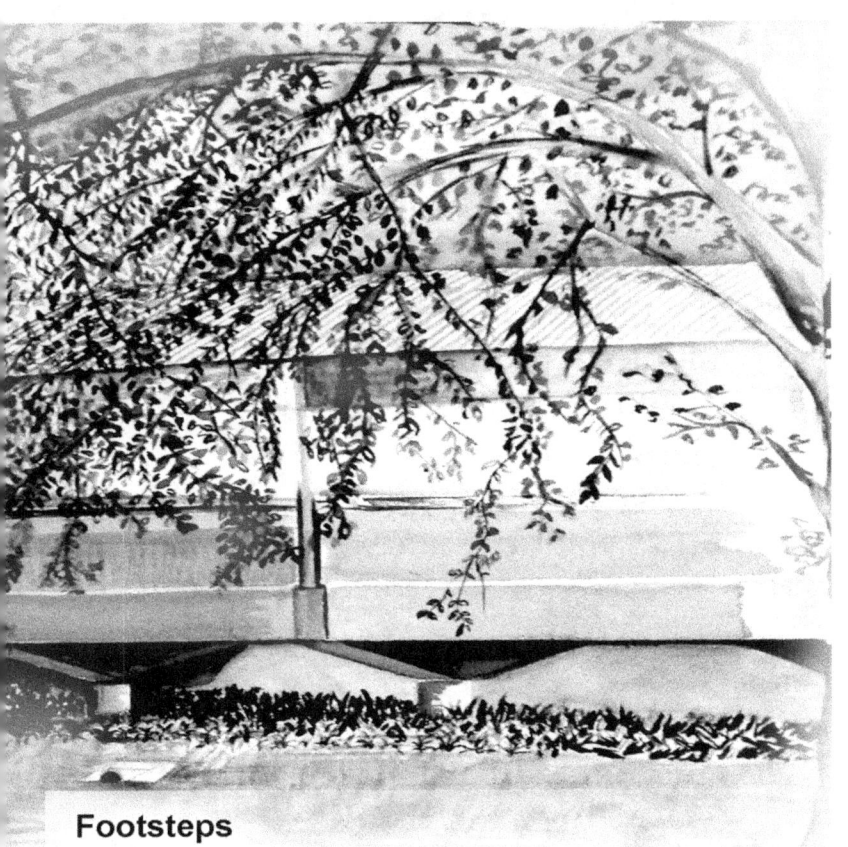

Footsteps

Your footsteps lead me down this trail of tears
This path less taken, by souls that fear
The inner demons, one can't face
A hanging skeleton, found its place
Hiding behind the mask of shame
It's all your fault, you're the one I blame
You think it's roses, but we burn in the dark
Petals to ashes, when we lose our spark
The past is gone
But I still hear your steps
Reminding me always
We're the only ones left

I'm in a race to the top
Get out of my way
This may hurt a little
Sting and ache
It's time to shine
I'll block the blazing sun
Turn it to ashes
Don't need a gun
At my feet the light will sink
and I will rise, above the weak

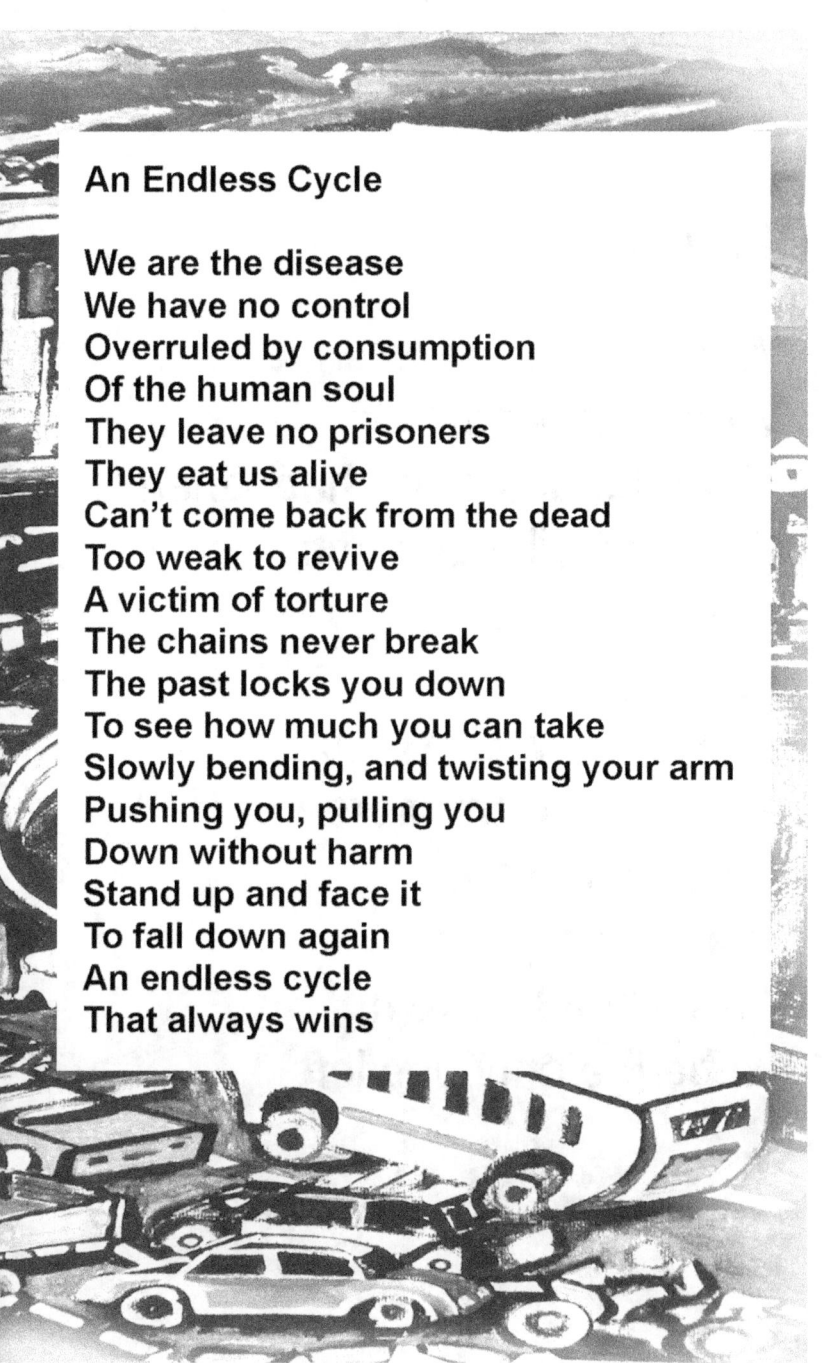

An Endless Cycle

We are the disease
We have no control
Overruled by consumption
Of the human soul
They leave no prisoners
They eat us alive
Can't come back from the dead
Too weak to revive
A victim of torture
The chains never break
The past locks you down
To see how much you can take
Slowly bending, and twisting your arm
Pushing you, pulling you
Down without harm
Stand up and face it
To fall down again
An endless cycle
That always wins

I'll be...

What horrors awake me
What will become
I'll pretend nothing happened
But who will succumb
Another terror
In this holy war
You'll know who I am
and you'll want more
No one to blame
But only myself
And when I wake up
I'll be the only one left

Broken

When things seem different
they're always the same
The truth is a monster
and we're all to blame

There's stars in our eyes
the light helps them glow
We're searching for angels
but they have broken souls

I'll grit my teeth and bare it
Soak it through my skin
Throw away the key
And hide it like a sin

It eats me up inside
To let go of my pride
Your footsteps trace my mind
Imprinting all your lies

Cold

You love to see me when I'm down
An easy target to push around
A smile so fragile it just might crack
on slippery ice we're sliding back

I can't hold on when you're so far away
Out of sight, out of mind
it hurts me to say

The pressure is building it's taking me down
and the ice might break if I make one sound
I'm holding it back I'm gritting my teeth
it's so hard to relax

I know I can't say it
but I want you to know
My heart's in a bind
because you're turning me cold

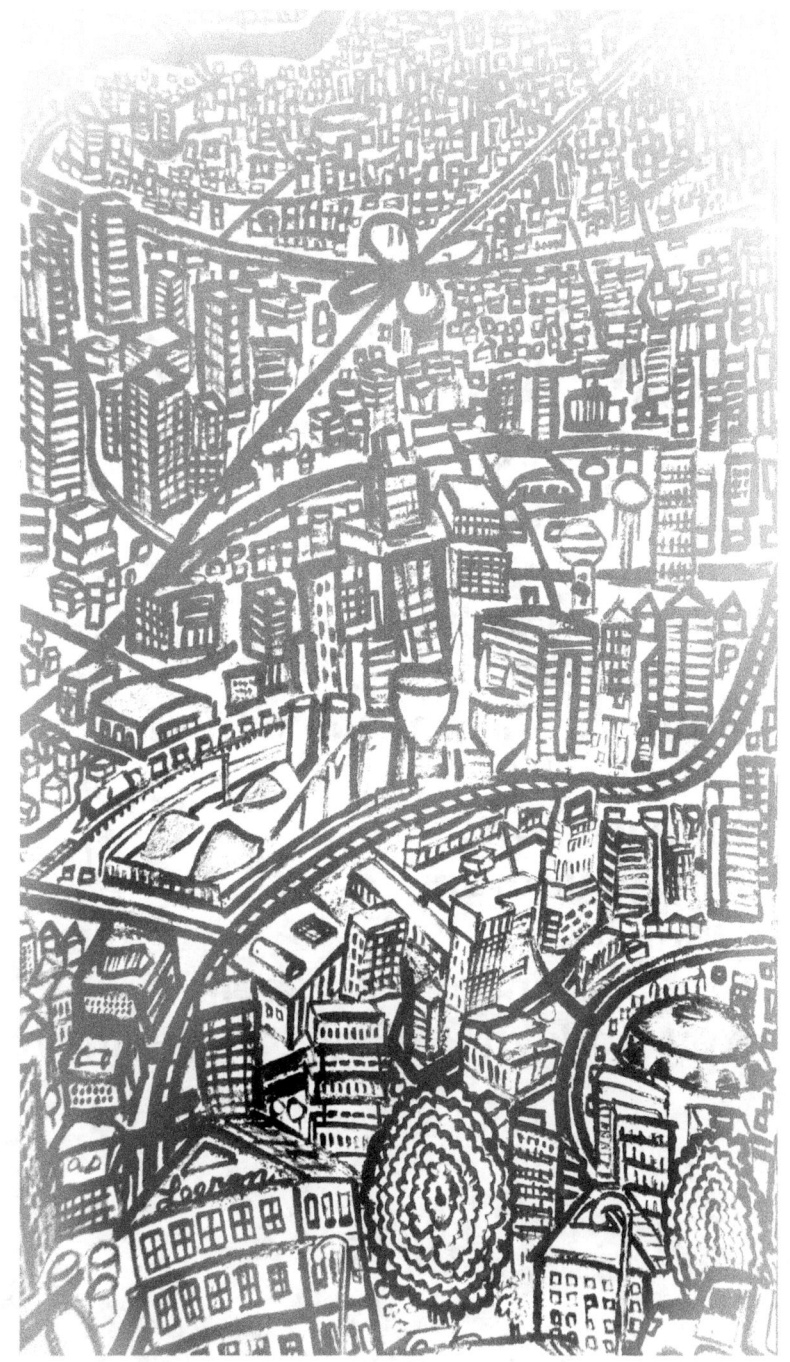

Gravity

You shape me
Mesmerize me
Into you

I fall through
Here I come
I'm sinking
Deeper, slowly
Don't wake me
From this dream come true

Intoxicate me
with your drug
Drink it down
Trapped under your spell
You work your magic on me again

You shake me
Twist and turn me
A carousel unscrewed
Here I come
I'm flying
You can't stop me
Gravity, where are you?

Perfect

I wish I could ease your pain
Catch every tear that made a stain
I wish I could give you every ounce of love
you ever needed
then I'd know that I succeeded
I'd be the happiest person alive
Just knowing I was perfect in your eyes
I'd smile and you'd smile back at me
And in your eyes I'd see
What I wish that we could be

Imperfection

If anyone's perfect—-it's you
and you're not
I used to believe you were
but when you stopped caring
my mind changed too
Everything you were was a lie
You were too good to be true
You were too perfect
But in the end I realize it was all an act
just so you could get what you wanted

as the surface is mutilated
those who still believe in inner beauty
will always stay true to what they love
no matter what

written by,
Allison Purifoy

INTERSECTION

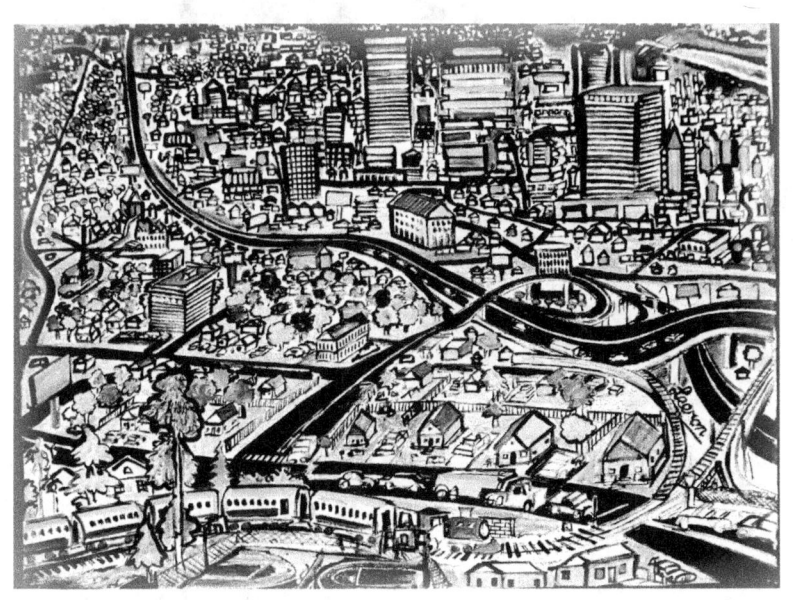

**illustrated by,
Leeron Morraes**

AT ROSE BLVD

WWW.BEANSPROUTBOOKS.COM

Morongo Valley, California

www.ingramcontent.com/pod-product-compliance
Lightning Source LLC
Chambersburg PA
CBHW052059110526
44591CB00013B/2280